MAPS OF TIME

MOSHE DOR

with an introduction by
ALAN SILLITOE

poems translated from the Hebrew by
JOHN BATKI, KEITH BOSLEY
RUTH FAINLIGHT, ELAINE FEINSTEIN
FRANCIS LANDY, DENIS JOHNSON
ANTHONY RUDOLF and ALAN SILLITOE
with the collaboration of the author

THE MENARD PRESS
LONDON 1978

MAPS OF TIME: poems in translation

Copyright © 1978 The Menard Press on behalf of
translators and the author

introduction
copyright © 1978 Alan Sillitoe

Hebrew poem on page
copyright © 1978 Hakibbutz Hameuchad Publishing House
who published the book, *Mapot Hazman,* from which most of the
poems included here are taken

Acknowledgements:
some of these translations first appeared in:
Greenfield Review, I.W.P., Jewish Chronicle, Jewish Quarterly,
Modern Poetry in Translation, South Dakota Review,
Tribune, Triquarterly
and in the anthology *The Burning Bush (W. H. Allen, 1977)*

We acknowledge the financial assistance of the
Institute for the Translation of Hebrew Literature Ltd.

All Rights Reserved

ISBN 0 903400 34 0

The Menard Press is a member of ALP

USA and Canada distribution by
Serendipity Books Distribution,
1636 Ocean View Avenue, Kensington, California 94707, USA

The Menard Press
23 Fitzwarren Gardens
London N19 3TR

Printed by Skelton's Press Ltd.
Wellingborough Northamptonshire

MAPS OF TIME

Rare Books
Room
PJ
5054
D6 M3613
c.1

CONTENTS

Introduction by Alan Sillitoe

The Leaves of the Olive Tree *(Elaine Feinstein)*	9
Among the Pine Trees *(Elaine Feinstein)*	10
Lips are Reluctant to Speak *(Alan Sillitoe)*	11
The World Shrinks *(Alan Sillitoe)*	12
Slow but Sure *(Alan Sillitoe)*	13
A Flood-Tide faces us *(Alan Sillitoe)*	14
Small Bones Ache *(Ruth Fainlight)*	15
Bottles *(Ruth Fainlight)*	16
A Dull Biography *(Ruth Fainlight)*	17
She is right, you know *(Moshe Dor)*	18
She is Right, you know *(Ruth Fainlight)*	19
Writing in a Notebook *(Keith Bosley)*	20
Slowly the Edges Change *(Keith Bosley)*	21
Transparent through the Window *(Keith Bosley)*	22
Tonight we'll be Bright and Clear *(Keith Bosley)*	23
An Aeroplane Scrawls Numerals *(Anthony Rudolf)*	24
A Park *(Anthony Rudolf)*	26
Fundamentals *(John Batki)*	26
Land's End, Cornwall *(Francis Landy)*	27

(the following poems are all translated by Denis Johnson)

The Dwelling	28
Going Back	29
Progression	30
War	31
A Demented Tree	32
In a Courtyard	33
Does David still Play before You	34
Wounds	35
Notes for an Armenian Biography	36
Morning	38
News of You	39
Train	40
From the Red-Tiled Rooftop	41
Birds	42
Green Idle Waters	44
Biographical Note on the author	46

INTRODUCTION

IN one of his poems Moshe Dor puts the question:
> 'How many bottles has he launched till now, while
> he still had the paper
> and ink, before the pen failed?'

That bottle, with its vital message, makes erratic lines across the world-map of experience, and elicits from a multiplicity of perils the eternal question as to what life itself means.

From the beginning to the end of his days no poet can afford not to ask that question. Nor can any poet expect a final answer. It would not be possible, anyway. Each poet makes a different song, fills in the flesh-and-blood of the question in his own way. That is what matters. God (for want of a better definition) preserves us from ever perceiving the answers which may turn out to be self-destroying, but instead embellishes the poet's questions so that he gets as close to the truth as possible.

The questions are eternal, and always more profound than any answers: perhaps peace, perhaps war, perhaps life, perhaps death. There is no way to avoid them (and no wish to do so in these poems) simply because it is impossible to get a final answer. It is necessary to take the questions head-on, or risk getting nowhere.

A poet is measured according to his complexity, and also by the simplicity with which he attempts to come to terms with complicated questions. Through his poems a good poet causes his readers to question the nature of all things in life. He peels back the very skin of consciousness in those who peruse him. He is a witch-doctor with words, a syntactical shaman, a priest of the perceptions.

He is also someone who matches the themes of life and death with the climate and topography of the earth. The nature of the land which the poet inhabits sets him apart, while his connection as a poet with the rest of the world does not suffer.

These poems are particularly significant because they come from Moshe Dor, and out of Israel via the Hebrew tongue. Percolating through translation into English, they have a long way to travel, though not as long as one might think, because such an itinerary has been previously followed and fundamentally explored.

Israel is a country which, for obvious reasons, is eternally lodged in the imagination of those who have any feeling for the English language. There is a sort of pipeline under the ocean of the spirit which connects all places where English and Hebrew are spoken. This book helps to bridge a gap, which some may still have to cross, between the great Hebrew poets of old, and those new poets of Modern Israel. Moshe Dor is one of them. One can only read the poems and give oneself up to the unique experience of his vision—and then judge whether or not one comes out richer in spirit.

Alan Sillitoe

THE LEAVES OF THE OLIVE TREE

The leaves of the olive tree open
like sails in the wind, and often
they are more silver than green
and sometimes greener,
when I look at them I must
disturb their balance,
they are no longer sails then
but become eyes of children
who long to cross green and silver seas
and never can
since their grey eyelashes have been
closed, and they wither in hiding.

AMONG THE PINE TREES

Among the pine trees
the voice of a dove as thin
feet run over cones, the countryside listens
with joy until

the first shot, then the next. A burst of shooting.

And there are figures taller than birds.
All birdsong muffled in their cries.
Silenced in the soft blue breath of their dying.

Thin and red are the feet of a dove
over needles and cones.

The countryside listens to the pause
and waits for sounds that wandered once
over pine-tree tops and can no longer
be heard.   Although we listen sadly.

LIPS ARE RELUCTANT TO SPEAK

Lips are reluctant to speak a single
word of love.
Pain reaches even the fingertips
when thunder clatters, or a bursting shell
fragments the pale horizon.
The aerials of the breeze continually comb
the tangled brush. It is the start of summer,
perhaps the last of spring, a dry
distress carrying neither the code
nor the key to it, in which
the lips are reluctant to speak
even a single word of love.

THE WORLD SHRINKS

The world shrinks against me. Morning
and evening close the limits of desire. A breeze
stops at the shoreline.

Why, world, do you shrink
like a withered orange?

Child, under
the tarmac lies a plot of earth
with oleanders and the smell of running water.
The whiteness of your beard increases, your hands
are thin, and still you wait.

SLOW BUT SURE

Slow but sure the insane light
transforms itself to sanity. So
autumn comes, followed by winter.
Even heretics give thanks
over the radiant balm. The sea has pulled
a long way back. The copper has dimmed. Thunder
lurks in its tunnels.

Slow but sure a painter
paints the white on whitewashed walls. Flecks
of white pepper my beard. The light
is delicate as if after paralysis. Thunder
like an express train will charge out of tunnels:
fear will strike no man, nor dolphin, the honey
dimming like amber too ancient
to be remembered.

A FLOOD-TIDE FACES US

A flood-tide faces us. Do not
put us to the test: our ears are seashells, seaweed
and sand between our toes. A flood-
tide faces us, the gull-screams fill
the spaces of our heart. Even if we
wanted to we couldn't hear. A flood-tide
faces us, and the cities spread behind. Do not
put us to the test, transient children like a passing shadow.
Our eyes are golden, a naked flame on
our flesh. The flood-tide
faces us and our cities
spread behind.

SMALL BONES ACHE

Small bones ache. A small
pain gnaws, needing no metaphors. A
country small in its love grows towards
hunger.

Nights' candles are no candles
for the night. A map carved in the bones
is not valid when examined. Small
bones ache.

Names are being obscured. Hunger nags. Pain
calls with the voice of a small turtle-dove. With
fingers of grease and dust
blind people trace countries of light upon
a map of skin.

Candles are extinguished. Small bones
ache.

BOTTLES

How many bottles has he launched till now, while
    he still had the paper
and ink, before the pen failed? Ripples on
the water like altering faces. From him to the
    unforgotten, the same
hurriedly-written note, tremblingly rolled, virgin before
sea-changes. How many
bottles floated, sunk, floated, reflecting
sun-glitterings from the glassy shelter, not
sensing the inner anguish? The palm-tree is dry,
    the beard
of the waiting one already curling against his hips,
salt-gnawed, channels
around his faded eyes. The scream
of the gull still turns every way as in the beginning, but
the tropical garden, surrounded by deeps, has only
    been a temptation
for tourists. He was immediately convinced of that.
    In
the few lines, repeated like an obsession,
he hasn't even made one reproach.
The light flows through his transparent
hands. Strange that weathering and sunburn have not
made them opaque, hands dropped lax in his lap.

A DULL BIOGRAPHY

Hard for light-bleeding eyes
to see in the dusky room.
And the year
is already the forty-second.

A dull biography: eyes that
bled light. A darkening room. The forty-
second year.

Forty two. The dykes of the body
crumble. The light is cruel,
pecking out eyes. A room
closes around its twilight.

Outside in the light, metals are proud
and indifferent to concepts: space, love,
time. In the room, everything is dimming
and crumbling. Indeed,
the forty-second.

Eyes of light being extinguished.
Metals also fatigue.

הצדק אתך את יודעת

הַצֶּדֶק אִתָּךְ, אַתְּ יוֹדַעַת, תָּלוּי בְּהֶחְלֵט
מֵהֵיכָן מִסְתַּכְּלִים. מִכָּאן
רוֹאִים תָּמָר, בֵּית אָדָם-רְעָפִים, קָמוּר מִזְרָחִי
וְשׁוּם רַבְקוֹמוֹת, כְּאִלּוּ שְׁמוּרַת
זִכָּרוֹן. וְהַיּוֹם ה-1 בְּדֶצֶמְבֶּר, וּבַחוּץ
מֶזֶג-אֲוִיר קֵיצִי. תִּהְיֶה
מִלְחָמָה, לֹא תִּהְיֶה. אַתְּ
אָמַרְתְּ, לִפְעָמִים דַּי שֶׁתִּהְיֶה לְאָדָם פִּסַּת
שָׁמַיִם, לֹא עוֹד, וּבְשׁוּפָרוֹ שָׁם יִתְקַע
הַמַּלְאָךְ גַּבְרִיאֵל. אֵינֶנִּי מַכִּיר שְׁמוֹת
מַלְאָכִים, אַדְווֹת זִכָּרוֹן בִּזְמַן שָׁקוּף
וּמֶזֶג-הָאֲוִיר קֵיצִי בָּ-1 בְּדֶצֶמְבֶּר. לֹא
יֵאָמֵן. תָּמָר, בֵּית אָדָם-רְעָפִים, קָמוּר
מִזְרָחִי וְשׁוּם רַבְקוֹמוֹת. וּמִלְחָמָה, אוּלַי
כֵּן, אוּלַי לֹא. קוֹל הַתּוֹר כְּמוֹ
קוֹל הַשּׁוֹפָר. אַתְּ
אָמַרְתְּ. רַק פִּסַּת שָׁמַיִם וּמְלֵאָה
כַּנְפֵי מַלְאָכִים. הַצֶּדֶק
אִתָּךְ. תָּלוּי מֵהֵיכָן מִסְתַּכְּלִים.

SHE IS RIGHT, YOU KNOW

She is right, you know. It definitely depends
on your point of view. From here
you see a date tree, a red-tiled house, an arabesque
and no block of flats, as if a memory-
reserve. And today is December 1, and outside it is
summery weather. There will be
war perhaps, no, there will not. She
said: Sometimes it is enough to have a plot
of sky, nothing more, and just there the angel Gabriel
will blow his horn. I don't know names
of angels. Ripples of memories in a transparent time
and summery weather on December 1. Incredible.
A date tree, a red-tiled house, an
arabesque and no block of flats. And war, perhaps
yes, perhaps no. The voice of the turtle-dove like
the voice of the horn. She
said. Only a piece of sky and full
of angels' wings. She is
right. It depends on your point of view.

WRITING IN A NOTEBOOK

Out from the olives, through the dusty green,
the breeze bears the dates of absolute justice,
before the reckoning and after.
I write in a notebook: After noon, about 2,
I saw a hare skipping towards the wild wheat;
at 2.17 a tortoise;
and a partridge — I didn't note the time — running in terror.
Plenty of observations for a nature-lover;
I am left empty-handed.

And next day there were the military exercises.
The children had serious faces,
they went down as instructed to the shelters, came out as instructed
to cultivated land, sweet air, the price of victory.
I write in a notebook: Before noon, about 8.30,
I saw a child running for cover in the belly of reinforced concrete
at 8.47 he was free;
and a woman — I didn't note the time — running in terror.
Plenty of qualms for a humanitarian;
I am left, as usual, empty-handed.

SLOWLY THE EDGES CHANGE

Slowly the edges change to stone. Maybe
the blood is tired of making
its round. Maybe Jerusalem
presses its aging body on Tel
Aviv with longings that fulfil
its ends. Jasmin
will sweeten stony rims, pine
will perfume lattices. Slowly
times and places change, necks
of camels and aircraft. Already the head
looks chiselled. Still the fingers
sing.

TRANSPARENT THROUGH THE WINDOW

Transparent through the window
and bright, the first rain falls.
The earth has heavy hips,
it sinks into her.

Slowly I watch. The fingers
of my right hand open and out of them
a book drops. The first
rain falls. Bright
the window and on the back
of the armchair, so transparent and light
death's hand rests.

Beyond the window the earth
is heavy and her hips ripen.
I shall sink into her.

TONIGHT WE'LL BE BRIGHT AND CLEAR

Tonight we'll be bright and clear on the coastal plain.
At noon the wind still shakes leaden birds, still
the rain with a blind man's grey fingers feels
the face of the earth.

The wind winds us up. Below the face of the earth
bulbs of rare flowers ripen. In spring
they will rise from dead men's eyes. Their names are lost
in the wind and it goes round and round.

Out of a blind man's opened fingers birds
of lead drip on the face of the earth. It is still
noon, foolish heart, be heavy
in my breast as a lump of lead. On the coastal plain
night lingers. Cold and bright, names
of rare flowers rise
from dead men's eyes, maybe
already on the mountains, maybe with the wind.

AN AEROPLANE SCRAWLS NUMERALS

An aeroplane scrawls numerals
higher than any arithmetic.
They look like milk
and I cannot decode them.
It is midsummer;
my friend says the nights are
cooler than ever,
the days
more humid than ever.

He may be right.
The air is
being polluted and,
like a woman's face, the land
changes its faces.
I sense how
    the ravines coagulate,
    the limestone yellows,
    the stucco peels off in strips,
    the water melon's meat
    grows pale, the sea retreats
    in fog, the big houses
    grow bigger and shake
    the horizon in their fangs.

My eyes strain
to tears and the aeroplane
still scrawls milky numerals;
their riddle remains unsolved.
My friend, it is midsummer,
a vein throbs in your temple and
still we have not been delivered.

A PARK

An old Englishman feeds birds
in St. James' Park:
sparrows and pigeons are
nourished in his hand.
His fingers are
almost still, the pale sun
enters the transparent skin,
the rustle of feathers,
like a small sea licking
the edges of
a life.

I also feed birds
in St. James' Park:
I fail:
my fingers are
too shaky and my skin
too foreign, though pale
now in the waters
of this sun;
a paper I read this morning
rustles in my eyes,
my stubborn oriental
wars pursue me.
It's a well known fact
that birds
shy away from nervous
people.

FUNDAMENTALS

This morning a train gave a long blare
and the fingers taking the pen trembled as if holding a snake.
Victories are not as simple as newspaper headlines
and the empty sleeve, the wounded sight
will not be replaced by shouting 'On your feet! Get going!'
Will you turn right or left, will you put on
a fur hat, will the beating of your heart alarm
your ears, like a sea?
I saw a pine and a cypress entwined
when the snow's love was crushing their branches.
The snow thawed and was forgotten and the trees stayed embraced
half brown withered death,
half life greener than ever.
This morning a train gave a long blare
and the fingers taking the pen trembled as if holding a snake.
The tongue was stumbling over heavy syllables
as if it was groping for long lost landmarks.
It is no longer possible to pin a sun on the breast
like a red flower. The white-hot light scorching
the eyes and the victors' vehicles imprinting
mechanized patterns on dirt roads.
At night they tossed in their sleep, huddled under army blankets,
and like children, they learned by heart the fundamentals:
               this is a star ..... this is a stone ....
this is my body breathing ......

LAND'S END. CORNWALL

Land's End.
A step, and already the infinite
blues, greens, greys, gull-shivering, torn by cries.
Perhaps from this rock were seen,
breaking the fog, Israelite ships.
Perhaps on sombre Semitic hair
clung tenuous salts.
Now a chance tourist
emits names of honey and milk,
promises of a lost land
on arid lips.
A step, and the hope of retreat
is the cry of gulls, beyond the reach of language,
deeper than memory. Land's
End, edge. No
further.

THE DWELLING

on alien ground I dwelt and also
I ate on the Day of Atonement unatoned
not even heretic my
eyes are rubies my mouth beaten gold
purple the thread in my beard

I am lord over 127 provinces
and frost in my bones spreads and pitch
plasters my palms

when I determined to build an ark
in order myself to escape on
alien ground a dark bird
cried his dark voice

I did not learn his name as I sank to the depths
my eyes they are rubies my mouth beaten gold
and purple the thread in my beard
a day of atoning for sin
I have not even yet fearlessly
set forward my heresy there is no faith
in my bones I am lord
127 provinces

I wept remembering Zion in the cold
when kingdoms
fall and dark are the wings of the bird
its cries a sea
of darkness I do not know my name

GOING BACK

According to the landmarks
I had come back to my starting line:
a gas station, a wounded olive trunk,
a ruined stone house.

Only your face
is not recognisable,
I shut it in my palms, deeply gazing.
Did we meet sometime? Sleep together?
Did I speak to you horrible,

loving words?
A gas station, wounded olive trunk, ruined stone house
do not strive to be more than they are,
but your face, breathing between my palms,

breaks some dark continuum
of which the naming
would be the naming also of myself, my true mission.
I can sleep beside you here,
from gas station to olive trunk to stone house
and when I awake, the seventy years
we are condemned to will be finished
and I no wiser than I was and
you no more open than you were
and all the deep slumbering
in the world will not have smoothed
even one wrinkle in my life, even one
storm between your breasts.

PROGRESSION

Even more terrible than crumbling, the dark
feeling of niches, the jokes
of purposeless entrances and exits,
the conflagration
of maple leaves like a forewarning:
but to keep silent?
A temporary solution, the memory of your body,
and more limited, of your breast,
its nipple standing up between two hungers,
my lips, words that are moaned, loss
of the pre-eminence of man,
and animal swept by the primeval ....
but to keep silent?
Maple leaves burn, too foreign
to scream, the hand ages on the
steering wheel, wild horses will not stop
the attrition of cells, seeds, hopes.
A meadow and a lakeside: the drawled speech
of fishers-for-sport drags lead nets
through opaque waters. But to keep silent?
Even more terrible than crumbling, the sudden
consciousness that when a star
sears these fabricated skies
no one looks up, for the change in it;
The car doors will slam,
an odour, faint, of smoke, then nothing.

WAR

> A light wind began blowing and brought
> from a neighbouring field many flowers that
> rained down all over the army until they
> found themselves dripping with bouquets.
>
> *Plutarch*

In his helmet he is a black rose
growing toward battle where the flowers of blood
will engulf his eyes. Now only the blaze
out of his green youth turns his cheeks red.

The scabbard trembles to be emptied as the war
engages the colour of a sexual fantasy:
there is no current inventory of his desire,
we know only that he waits patiently, voluptuously

for the singing of horns. From where he stood
the sling-stones, turning golden in the light,
seemed chrysanthemums lost from his childhood
and his shock at the sudden pain was slight.

The scribbled inventory of those hurt
— their numbers, units, living relations —
listed him among the first, and in the curt
military style offered itemization
of what he had that was theirs to take back.

In such epic cataloguing of the gear
and gashes of batallions there is some lack
of attention to poetry — sad, for it was clear

at the opening of battle that he was a black rose
and even clearer — blacker, more like a flower — at the close.

A DEMENTED TREE

A demented tree
growing in a crumbling house.
The top branches
have already burst the roof, toward
conjectured skies, possible to define
no more than the tree is possible to name.
A demented tree whose
roots already gnaw the floor,
sucking up memories, the lost
lust, dusty heartbreaks.
A totally demented tree:
in fact the crumbling is perhaps
a desire of the bark, a fermentation
of the sap, a quivering
that will not release my fingers
when the skin craves the security
of your nakedness like a stripped house
longing for its wallpaper,
for the secrecy of curtains,
for a door shut against
the greenish, savage goring by stars.

IN A COURTYARD

In the courtyard the children play hide-and-seek.
Sunset is red in the few trees.
Already poetry is meaningless.
The street is unpaved and proud in its dirt.
A boy on a bicycle rushes toward desperate missions.
There is no one in the locked office of the heart
to say for certain you are coming.

In the court the children lie down with their eyes closed.
A white moon pours mourning glass on their eyelids.
The evening editions announce the boy was run over
going toward the horizon.
I know, like love, the name of the killer
and that the bicycle was not damaged.
That behind bars sleep would be dreamless,
even the open veins would be beautiful.

DOES DAVID STILL PLAY BEFORE YOU

Does David still play before you
on the golden harp?
And Solomon,
does he still invent, in your hearing,
his fox fables?

And from which field does Elijah take off
in a chariot of fire and with horses of fire?
and Ezekiel,
what being hammers him, with what creature
does he struggle in the stormy, shining substance?

And among curls of incense,
does still to forgive and love
plead the face, paler than a cloud,
of Jesus, with the Yellow Star?

And from out which savage Bible
of erupting, extinguished suns
do your hands, hardened
in the arteries, grope regretfully to tear
up disappointed promises?

WOUNDS

> Una cancion es una herida de amor
> que nos abrieron las cosas.
> *Gabriela Mistral*

The wounds of love
are healed.
The words
will be dulled.
The voice
will not make itself heard.

The wounds of metal
are real.
The withering
flower of someone's manhood
is flung across the wide starlessness.
The torn chest clutches
the flare-bomb, the words
retreating, stumbling, their eyes scarred.

The wounds of love have knit.
The wounds
of metal are fresh, the blood is like dew,
golden nightingales will grow calm
emerging from the storm in the arteries,
fluttering over the white virginity of bone.
The words will move into twilight.

NOTES FOR AN ARMENIAN BIOGRAPHY

The zodiac does not encircle
the head of Astrik Bartevian, Armenian,
tailor, thin, large-eyed, sewing
his life into stitches here in

his home, an alley wholly
stone: not a river, no poplars
on its banks, and the old language
patch on patch. His chest sinks

as if he leans permanently to meditate
on hopelessness. He does not want payment
when the needle flies over the trousers.
The king does not pitch his tent

by the river, there even the eyes
of the crucified one become stones.
Sometimes, talking to the whore from
down the alley, listening more than speaking.

he flares slightly his nostrils
into the sweet dark perfume. A
very lonely man, who once dreamed
he weaved gold brocade for the arch-bishop's robe,

forgetting the elemental dictum of blackness,
who once in his dreaming sailed the boat
of the moon home, where he had never been,
where he wept between white peaks while

the grass flared like a green madness
on those slopes. Astrik
Bartevian, Armenian, when the thunderhead
of bells tears open around him, gives

thanks that his fate is ordained,
that he lives in a holy city and sews
with decaying fingers shrouds
for little stone birds.

MORNING

Here is another clear morning descending
to pluck figs in the sun's orchards,
another golden furrow opened
in Father's high forehead.
Gather flocks
to the pastures in the sky
and we shall feel the shade, green, fertile,
as little bells jingle in our eyes.

And from the edges of the Bible,
silently, birds drop to pick
red berries from the breast of the young shepherd
whose reflection is a seal on the heart of the stream.

NEWS OF YOU

A hand, stretched over vast waters,
gathers in its palm flowing fog.
The announcer
intones numbers, facts, his voice
precise in setting a limit
to speculations. But the fingers palpitate,
feeling fog, remembering
like strokes of electricity your thighs
opening, flowing pleasure.

Words go on,
kites held by strings
of laughter and weeping, prisoners
to earth. The fog covers the face of the waters,
grey expanses of groping,
the announcer is precise, mentioning names, events,
the fingers
drop glittering copper birds on
the soil's naked belly.

A fog of birds' wings.
Their one voice pours
from the knots of kites to fertilize
a mute pleasure
and make it flower.

TRAIN

In the beginning the blare of a train.
And from out of the thick
of forests, mountains, blue smoke
of foreign parts, pale fire, the whole complex
mosaic of pain-misted existences,
your face drifts and crystallizes.
Secret beloved: so again I study the map
of the face, learning
by heart the country of my longing. The smell
of crushed eucalyptus leaves,
yellowing grass, clear shreds of glass
that reflect a cloud, an aircraft, and again
the blare of a train. Autumn opaques with belts
of red and orange the depth and the distance, your
face, the shade of eyelashes.
One must browse
in a new dictionary, looking
for names for forests, mountains, the blue
smoke of foreign parts, pale fire,
but it is impossible for ten brittle fingers
to suppress a sudden shudder,
to turn a page, another page
as if no train blares in time and space
and in its stubborn wisdom, knowing the cold estimates.

FROM THE RED-TILED ROOFTOP

From the red-tiled rooftop
I see
how fog swaddles
the opposing hills in
its cool breath. A soft
winter
solstice containing no
thoughts of regret
is dropping on the television antennas,
the poplars sway
in rhythm and below, beautiful, golden-haired Chloe
with a baby carriage
is passing by, sparks of smoke in her hair.

Hush, town and universe,
let there be
peace
in this neutral fog
until all antennas receive
and broadcast the red, tall pictures of my heart
to the veiled hills and to
golden-haired Chloe below,
in whose baby carriage the future sun is sleeping.

BIRDS

Two Hungarian women are speaking
Hungarian at Café Peter.
They slowly float, their eyes filling
with another, a Hungarian, time.
The stones of the café pity them
delicately in a Palestinian slang
mixed with Turkish.
Also the casuarinas

at Café Peter send to accompany them
their tall pity, bird-murmured.
But seated under the casuarinas I
pity even more the birds,
who carry on confused wings
my own time, and can't think how
to get rid of it.
Why did you yield
to the impulse of your birdliness, why
now are you so confused, heavy
with dark, unbirdlike meanings trembling
within themselves, refusing
to become plumage, or a beat of the small
heart, a vital twitter?
Now the birds

have grown silent,
the Hungarian women have sailed off
on a Danube of glittering,
receding lights. Only
the cuckoo-clock is not quiet. Something
troubles it in the fastnesses

of its own private time,
something not wood, not
cuckoo — the flutter
of a diagonal plume above a green gaze.
Silence, silence,
cuckoo-clock. Soon
we will begin our own journey at Café Peter
and end it in a fading face,
a forgotten echo, a long, blue wait
deepening in its blueness
before a gate whose keeper
will approach us in his own good time, holding
in his lap the stars — birds
from all the dreams we have ever held, or let go.

GREEN IDLE WATERS

> Ay, Guadalquivir!
> *F.G. Lorca*

Green, idle waters,
and in the plaza, Maimonides
sinks down into powerful thoughts,
his face
turned toward Tiberias of sound sleep
where the answers are.

From the East will come, not Magi,
but disgusting lechers to seduce dark women
with an oleander burning on each heart,
to uncover sweet nakednesses
and beget, among arches,
a dark hatred, horrible in metal mantillas
and sharply pointed hoods.

MOSHE DOR

Moshe Dor was born in 1932 in Tel Aviv where he completed his elementary and secondary education and joined the Haganah as a young man. He served as correspondent of the Israel Army weekly magazine *Bamahaneh*. He studied at the Universities of Tel Aviv and Jerusalem, and received his B.A. in Political Science and History.

He was one of the founder-members and editors of the 'Likrath' group, which comprised many of the most important young writers of the early fifties and promulgated the 'New Manner' in Hebrew Letters, His first collection of poems was published by *Likrath* in 1954. He has since published nine more books of poetry, three collections of children's verse, a collection of literary essays and a book of interviews with foreign writers visiting Israel, including W.H. Auden, Guenter Grass, Miguel Angel Asturias, and others — as well as interviews with Israeli writers. He has translated several works, by English and American writers, among them Robert Graves's *The Golden Fleece*, Anthony Hope's *The Prisoner of Zenda* and Jack London's *Odyssey in the North*.

Moshe Dor works as a journalist. Since 1958, he has been on the editorial board of *Maariv* . He represented Israel in 1970–71 at the International Writing Program of the University of Iowa. He has served on the central board and presidium of the Hebrew Writers' Union and is a member of Israel's Press Council and the P.E.N. Club. From 1975–1977 he was Counsellor for Cultural Affairs at the Embassy of Israel in London.

Moshe Dor is married and has two sons.